CI
IN

*"Describe Christmas in three words."*

That was the challenge put to various celebrities in a television advertising campaign a few years ago.

Answers included: *"Last-minute shopping"*, *"Eating too much"* and *"Filling a stocking"*. What would you say? *"Holly and ivy"* perhaps? Or *"family and friends"*?

But what about the words, *"Christ is born"*? Where do they fit in?

It's easy at Christmas time to be so preoccupied with shopping and partying that we forget what it is we're supposed to be celebrating. The Bible describes the coming of Jesus as an event of massive significance for God's dealings with the world he made, and for every individual in it.

I have chosen my own three words to summarise the Bible's teaching about the true meaning of Christmas: *"historical"*, *"joyful"* and *"essential"*. Those words point to truths that have transformed the lives of millions of people throughout the world... they could transform your life too.

# 1. Christmas is historical: it really happened

Many people think of Jesus in the same category as Santa, Rudolph the red-nosed reindeer and a magic snowman. We've known the story of his birth in the manger since childhood. We may have believed in it then, but now that we've reached the adult world of harsh reality. Don't we have to face facts and accept that, just as Father Christmas doesn't really live at the North Pole, so Jesus wasn't really born in a manger?

No! The Bible insists that Jesus is not just a mythical character; he really existed. The best way to find out more about him is to read one of the Gospels in the New Testament of the Bible. They were all written within a few decades of the events they describe and take great care to record accurate history.

Luke, for example, begins his Gospel by describing the efforts he has taken to ensure he has got his facts right: 'carefully investigating everything' and receiving his information from 'eyewitnesses'.

The New Testament is not a myth or fantasy; it's history. Jesus *really was* born in a stable in Bethlehem. He then grew up to become the most remarkable man the world has ever seen. One writer has put it well:

**I'm far within the mark when I say that all the armies that ever marched, and all the navies that ever sailed,**

**and all the parliaments that ever sat, and all the kings that ever reigned, put together, have not affected the life of man upon earth as has that one solitary life.**

There has never been anyone else like Jesus. He lived a life of astonishing humility, kindness and compassion. He loved everyone: rich and poor, male and female, Jew and Gentile. He taught as no one else has ever taught.

Although he was an unschooled carpenter from an obscure part of the Roman Empire, his words still captivate the minds of millions two thousand years after he lived on earth. And he performed extraordinary miracles, which even his enemies couldn't deny. He just said the word and the blind saw, the lame walked and the dead were raised.

But, despite all the good he did, the religious establishment felt threatened by him and persuaded the Roman authorities to have him crucified when he was still only in his early thirties. If that was where the story ended, his brief life would have been largely forgotten by now, but he didn't stay in the tomb. God raised him from the dead and he appeared to many people. This was no ordinary man! And he is not a mythical or fictional character. Christmas is historical: it really happened!

## 2. Christmas is joyful: God really cares

Christmas is not just historical; it's also joyful. An angel who had been sent by God announced the birth of Jesus to some shepherds saying: *"I bring you good news of great joy that will be for all the people"*. But what is the joyful message of Christmas?

Harrods, the department store in London, put these words in their Christmas catalogue:

**Christmas is coming, joyful and triumphant in a blaze of splendour. Harrods is brim full of comfort and joy, overflowing with grandeur. Let the glory of Christmas ring out!**

But does the glory and joy of Christmas really only consist of the goods in the shops? Christmas shopping has been likened to a tumble dryer: you go round and round in circles, get very hot, and when you arrive home you realise you've been taken to the cleaners. There must be more to Christmas than that!

The birth of a baby is always a time of rejoicing, especially for the family; but it's hard to get excited if we don't know the parents, and if the birth took place in another part of the world many centuries ago. So why should we rejoice at the birth of Jesus in Bethlehem?

The answer is because of who he is. The angel told the shepherds:

**"Today in the town of David a saviour has been born to you; he is Christ the Lord."**

God had acted to fulfil his promises made many years before through the prophets in the Old Testament:

**"The virgin will be with child and will give birth to a son, and they will call him Immanuel" – which means, "God with us".**

God is not a distant God; he loves us and has drawn near to us in the person of his Son, Jesus Christ.

Christmas is a natural time for us to look back on the year that has passed. Perhaps it has been a difficult one for you and God has felt a million miles away. You may be able to identify with the words of Sting's song, *"O my God"*:

**Everyone I know is lonely**
**And God's so far away**
**And my heart belongs to no one,**
**So now sometimes I pray**
**Please take the space between us**
**And fill it up some way.**

The great news is that God did exactly that on the first Christmas Day: he filled up the space between him and us. We still may not understand why there is so much suffering in the world, but at least we can be sure that God is not indifferent to it. He didn't simply send his condolences by long-distance phone call; he got involved by sending his own Son to be born on earth.

Jesus was fully divine, but he didn't protect himself from the harsh realities of life. He was born in a manger, not a mansion; rode a donkey, not a chariot; and was lifted onto a cross, not a throne. Christmas tells us that God loves us; why else would he have sent his Son to leave all the glory of heaven and be born as a man in the midst of the suffering of this world? That's a great reason to be joyful: God really cares!

## 3. Christmas is essential: it really matters

Jesus didn't just come to earth to demonstrate God's love; he came to achieve an urgent rescue. The apostle Paul, one of the greatest early Christian leaders, tells us:

**Christ Jesus came into the world to save sinners.**

When I first heard those words it didn't occur to me that they had any relevance for me. I assumed that the real sinners were other people: murderers, rapists and paedophiles. In my more humble moments I could admit I wasn't perfect, but I lived a fairly decent life and I assumed that, if there was a God, he approved of me. But then someone pointed out that the heart of sin is our attitude to God. None of us has lived in his world as we should.

Our behaviour is illustrated by the story of a little boy who had desperately wanted to play Joseph in the school nativity play but was given the more minor part of the inn keeper instead. Wounded, the boy sulkily waited for a suitable moment to take his revenge. On the night of the play, with the school hall packed with teachers and proud parents, Mary and Joseph came towards him and delivered their familiar line: "Is there any room at the inn?"

Instead of saying "no" and offering the stable, the boy saw his opportunity to steal the show and, with a broad smile replied, "Yes, plenty of room, come right in!" Poor Mary and Joseph stood dumbfounded, not knowing what to do next, and the production descended into chaos.

There's something of that boy in all of us. If all the world's a stage, then God our creator wrote the play, designed the set and is the producer as well. Our role is to live as he designed us to: in grateful, trusting submission to him. That is the best way to live, as the maker intended. But we're not happy with the part he has given us: it doesn't give us the prominence we think we deserve, so we tear up the script, writing our own lines with God pushed to the margins and ourselves at the centre.

Although he has been very generous and given us all the good things we enjoy—our families, friends, abilities and possessions—we rarely, if ever, say 'thanks'. We decide how we're going to live our lives and God hardly gets a look in, if he gets in the picture at all. That's what sin is: rejecting God's authority and living in his world as if he doesn't exist. The results are disastrous. We think we can improve God's play, but in fact we destroy it.

Human sin is the ultimate cause of all that spoils life on earth, leading to the oppression, injustice and warfare which blight the lives of millions. But the impact of sin is also seen very close to home. Why is it that Christmas is one of the most stressful periods of the year? Even at this time of 'peace and goodwill', we aren't able to suppress our selfishness and find it almost impossible to get on with those we love most.

Sin isn't just a problem for other people; it infects us all and destroys the perfect world God made. It is surely no surprise that the Bible says he is angry with us. A just God who cares about right and wrong can't just ignore our sin; he must punish it. The punishment we all deserve is eternal separation from him.

In his justice God must punish, but in his great love he longs to forgive us. That's why he sent Jesus to earth on the first Christmas Day: to rescue us so that we could be his friends again. Jesus lived a perfect life. He was the one man who ever lived who did not deserve to face the punishment of death and separation from God. But he willingly obeyed his heavenly Father, and stood in for sinful humanity when he died on the cross.

Jesus took the punishment we deserved, so we needn't face it. If we trust in him, we can be sure that the price has been paid for all our sins and we are completely accepted by God, not because of anything we've done, but because of Jesus' death in our place. We needn't fear the day when Christ returns to judge the world, but can instead look forward to joining him in the perfect new creation he will establish.

A few days before Christmas in 1991, nineteen-year-old Robin Farmer had just returned to Northern Ireland after his first term at university in Scotland. He was working in the family's shop in County Tyrone when a terrorist gunman burst in and aimed a gun at his father, who was a police reservist. Robin instinctively dived in front of his father and was hit instead, dying shortly afterwards. That courageous sacrifice reflects something of what Jesus did for us. As Robin's father can say, "My son died for me", so we can say, "God's Son died for us". That's why he had to come to earth. There was no other way by which we could be right with God and have our sins forgiven. Christmas is essential: it really matters!

## What will we do with the present?

There has never been a better Christmas present than God's gift of his own Son to be the saviour of the world.

**Christmas is historical.** We shouldn't treat it as just a story for the kids: *it really happened!*

**Christmas is joyful.** We can be sure that God loves us: *he really cares!*

**And Christmas is essential.** The coming of Jesus is not only relevant to religious people, or those with a Christian background. Jesus' rescue is the only hope of anyone being forgiven and accepted by God: *it really matters!*

So what will we do with the present?

Let's make sure we don't make the same mistake as Thelma Howard, an American maid, who missed out on a fortune because she didn't look carefully enough at her

Christmas present. Her employer was Walt Disney, who gave her a piece of paper in an envelope every Christmas Eve.

Thelma didn't understand what they were, so she simply added them to a pile under her bed. After her death her relatives discovered the documents and realised that they were shares in the Disney Corporation, worth thirty million dollars.

God's gift to us of his Son, Jesus Christ, is far more valuable than any sum of money. Even if you're not convinced that Jesus is God's Son, it's surely worth finding out more about him. You have nothing to lose, and you could have much to gain.

Why not read one of the New Testament Gospels for yourself? It would also help to find a church where your questions could be answered. Many churches organise *Christianity Explored, Alpha* or a similar course which helps people investigate the Christian faith.

But it may be that your questions have already been answered. All that's needed is for you to make a decision to stop keeping Christ at arm's length, and instead to trust him for forgiveness and begin to live for him as your Lord. That won't be easy, but you won't be on your own. Christ gives his Spirit to all his followers so that we can grow in our relationship with him and be equipped to serve him. There's no better way to live.

If you want to receive Christ and begin to follow him, you could use these words as your prayer to God. If you pray them, do tell someone else so you can receive the help you need as you start a whole new way of living.

> *Dear God*
>
> *Thank you for your great love in sending your Son Jesus to be born on earth. I confess that I have turned away from you and deserve your condemnation.*
>
> *I now trust in Jesus and his death on the cross as the only way by which I can be right with you.*
>
> *Please give me your Holy Spirit and strengthen me to serve you to the very end of my life, and then take me to live in your new creation forever.*
>
> *In Jesus' name*
>
> *Amen*